Volcano

Volcano

contents

Volcano
Fact Matters

ISBN-13: 978-1-4190-5468-6
ISBN-10: 1-4190-5468-6

First published by Blake Education Pty Ltd as *Go Facts*
Copyright © 2006 Blake Publishing
This edition copyright under license from Blake Education Pty Ltd
© 2010 Steck-Vaughn, an imprint of HMH Supplemental Publishers Inc.

All rights reserved. No part of the material protected by this copyright may be reproduced or utilized in any form or by any means, in whole or in part, without permission in writing from the Publisher. Requests for permission should be mailed to: Paralegal Department, 6277 Sea Harbor Drive, Orlando, FL 32887.

Steck-Vaughn is a trademark of HMH Supplemental Publishers Inc.

Printed in China

If you have received these materials as examination copies free of charge, HMH Supplemental Publishers Inc. retains title to the materials and they may not be resold. Resale of examination copies is strictly prohibited.

Possession of this publication in print format does not entitle users to convert this publication, or any portion of it, into electronic format.

2 3 4 5 6 7 8   0940   15 14 13 12 11 10

4	What Is a Volcano?
6	How Volcanoes Are Formed
8	Eruption! Why Do Volcanoes Erupt?
10	After the Eruption
12	Volcanoes of the World
14	Types of Volcanoes
16	Types of Eruptions
18	How to Make Your Own Volcano
20	Case Study—Mount St. Helens
22	Volcanic Landscapes
24	Living with Volcanoes
26	Working with Volcanoes
28	Time Line
30	Table, Glossary, and Index

What Is a Volcano?

The solid ground that we walk on is part of the Earth's **crust**. Below this crust lies a layer of **magma**. Magma is very hot, **molten** rock. When magma explodes through an opening in the Earth's crust, a volcano **erupts**.

Some volcanoes are cone-shaped mountains. Others are wide, sloping hills. They can also be under the ocean. Volcanoes form when molten rock from deep within the Earth breaks through the Earth's crust. Magma that reaches the surface is called lava.

Volcanoes and Us

Volcanoes can cause mudslides, floods, tsunamis, and fast-moving waves of hot, **poisonous** gases. Volcanoes are one of nature's most frightening and amazing events. They have a huge **impact** on the landscape. Land can be ruined for a long time after an eruption. Volcanoes bury towns. They create islands and mountains. They truly change the world.

Volcano Activity

Volcanoes that have erupted recently, or are likely to erupt soon, are called active. Dormant volcanoes haven't erupted for a long time but still could. Extinct volcanoes are no longer active.

About 550 volcanoes around the world are known to be active. Around 60 erupt every year.

Lava erupts at temperatures of up to 2,200 degrees Fahrenheit.

Volcanoes can generate amazing lightning storms. The lightning is caused by the friction between particles of rock and ash in the air.

Did You Know?

There are also volcanoes on other planets. The gigantic Olympus Mons on Mars is 13 miles high and 335 miles wide.

How Volcanoes Are Formed

Volcanoes occur when hot magma pushes its way through the Earth's crust. The Earth's crust is made up of separate pieces called tectonic plates. These plates fit together like a giant jigsaw puzzle. Most volcanoes form at the edges of these plates.

Colliding Plates

There are about 12 large tectonic plates and several smaller ones. All of them are moving. Underneath the Earth's crust is the **mantle**. Because the rock in the mantle is very hot, it gets soft. Sometimes it even melts. The tectonic plates move over this layer of hot rock.

Subduction Volcanoes

When tectonic plates **collide**, the heavier plate usually slides underneath the lighter one. This is called **subduction**. As the lower plate is pushed into the hot mantle, it melts and becomes magma.

Molten magma is lighter than the solid rock around it, so it slowly rises. **Pressure** from the rocks around it forces the magma to the surface. It breaks through weak or thin spots in the crust. This creates subduction volcanoes.

Spreading Ridges

A spreading ridge is where two tectonic plates move apart. Molten magma rises up into the opening. This creates new crust. Many spreading ridges occur under the ocean. They create undersea volcanoes.

Hot Spot Volcanoes

Hot spots are very hot areas in Earth's mantle. The hot magma breaks through the tectonic plate above it. As the plate moves, a chain of volcanoes is formed.

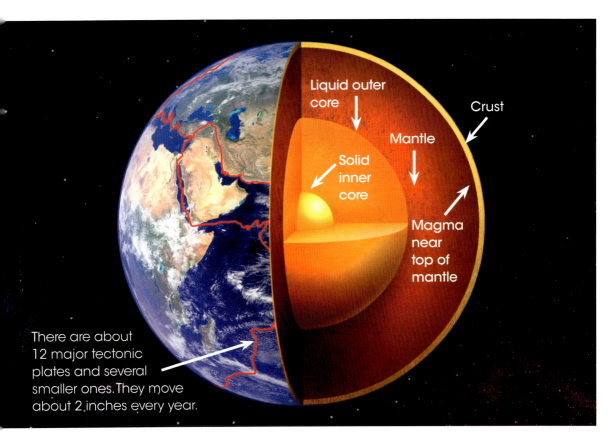

There are about 12 major tectonic plates and several smaller ones. They move about 2 inches every year.

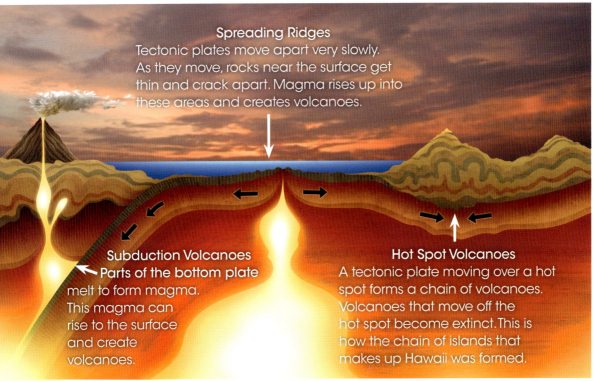

Spreading Ridges
Tectonic plates move apart very slowly. As they move, rocks near the surface get thin and crack apart. Magma rises up into these areas and creates volcanoes.

Subduction Volcanoes
Parts of the bottom plate melt to form magma. This magma can rise to the surface and create volcanoes.

Hot Spot Volcanoes
A tectonic plate moving over a hot spot forms a chain of volcanoes. Volcanoes that move off the hot spot become extinct. This is how the chain of islands that makes up Hawaii was formed.

Eruption! Why Do Volcanoes Erupt?

As magma rises, gases expand and water becomes steam. This creates a lot of pressure. When the pressure becomes too great, a volcano erupts. Eruptions can range from gentle oozing to violent **explosions.**

Magma collects in a **magma chamber** underneath a volcano over time. Molten magma is lighter than the rock around it, so it rises toward the surface. As it rises, gas bubbles begin to form. Finally, it erupts through one or more **vents**.

Viscosity

Eruptions can be smooth flows of lava or enormous explosions. This depends on the **viscosity** of the magma—how thick and sticky it is—and its gas content. When magma is very viscous and contains a lot of gas, the eruption will be explosive. This is because gases have trouble escaping from the thick magma. As magma rises, the gas expands. This causes great pressure. The pressure finally causes the magma to erupt violently through the vent.

When magma is less viscous, gas escapes more easily. This causes less violent eruptions. Once magma reaches the surface, it is called lava.

Volcanoes also cause terrifying and deadly **pyroclastic flows**. These are destructive clouds of boiling gas and ash. They explode out of the volcano and flow downhill at great speed. They destroy everything in their paths.

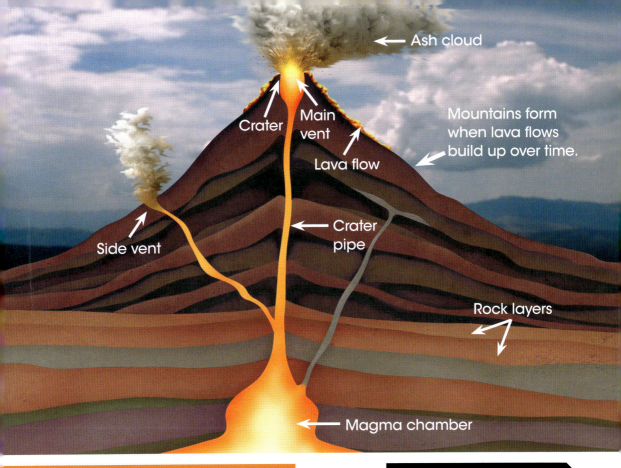

Ash cloud

Crater

Main vent

Lava flow

Mountains form when lava flows build up over time.

Side vent

Crater pipe

Rock layers

Magma chamber

Gas-rich magma is much more explosive than magma that contains less gas.

Did You Know?

Material from previous eruptions can block a volcano's vents. This builds up a lot of pressure inside the volcano. It can lead to explosive eruptions. When Mount St. Helens erupted in 1980, 300 million tons of material were thrown from the volcano.

After the Eruption

A volcanic eruption can cause falling ash, poisonous gases, and mudslides. These can have a powerful impact on people and the landscape.

Ash

Volcanic ash is like finely crushed glass. It blasts into the air as an eruption plume and falls back to Earth. It is not usually deadly by itself. But a thick layer can crush roofs and ruin crops.

Lahars

Volcanoes can cause **devastating** mudslides. These are known as **lahars**. Falling ash, soil, and rock combine with water and flow down volcanic slopes. The heat of an eruption can melt snow and cause lahars. The mix of melted snow, soil, and ash rushes downhill. This mix can swallow up houses and trees. In 1985 the Mount Ruiz volcano in Colombia erupted. It caused lahars that buried the town of Armero, killing 22,000 people.

Gas

Volcanic eruptions can release deadly gases, such as carbon dioxide and sulfur dioxide. Carbon dioxide is heavier than air. It collects in low areas and creates poisonous environments. Sulfur dioxide causes acid rain and air pollution.

A small amount of ash can fertilize soil. Too much will destroy plant life.

Did You Know?

When Mount Pinatubo in the Philippines erupted in 1991, it blocked out sunlight for days. About 300 people were killed.

In 1995 a rain of ash covered the city of Plymouth on the Caribbean island of Montserrat. Once a thriving capital, it is now a ghost town. The city is covered in more than a yard of volcanic ash.

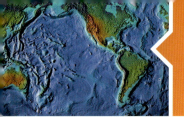

Volcanoes of the World

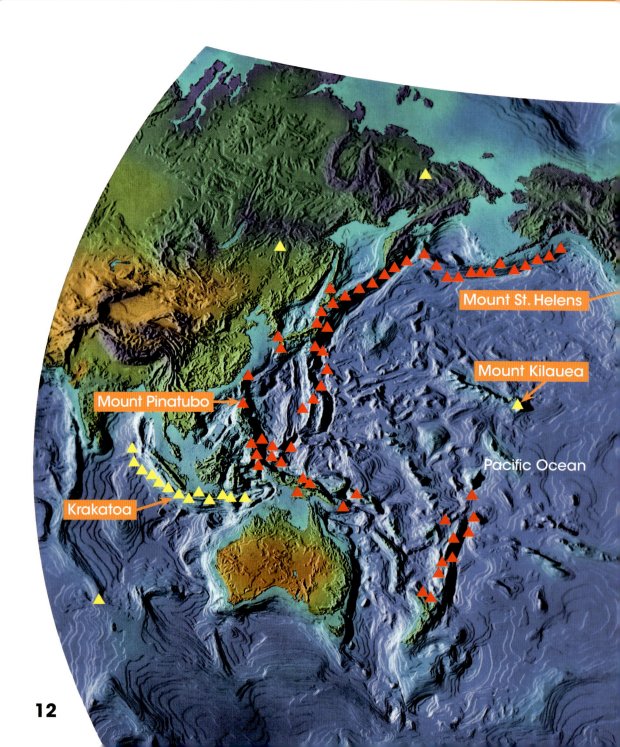

About two-thirds of the world's volcanoes are found in Africa, Europe, and the "Ring of Fire" around the Pacific Ocean.

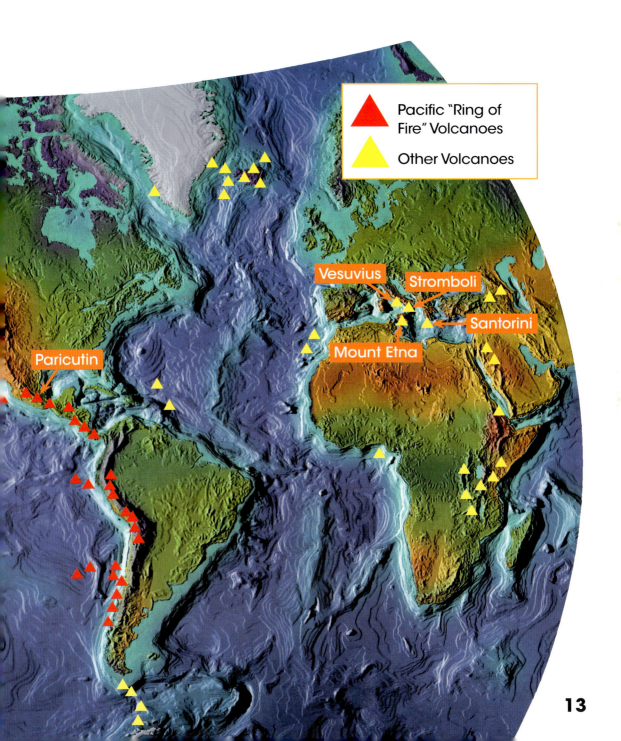

Types of Volcanoes

The four main types of volcanoes are composite, shield, **cinder** cone, and **caldera** volcanoes.

Composite Volcanoes

Composite volcanoes are made up of overlapping layers of lava and ash. They are also known as stratovolcanoes. Viscous magma traps gases and builds up pressure. This pressure finally causes violent eruptions, such as Plinian eruptions.

Shield Volcanoes

These largest of volcanoes mostly occur at spreading ridges and hot spots. Formed by thinner lava, they have gentle slopes and spread over large areas. They erupt every few years, creating lava flows and **lava fountains**. Hawaiian volcanoes are shield volcanoes. Their eruptions are called Hawaiian eruptions.

Composite volcanoes don't erupt often. Hundreds of years pass between eruptions.

Mauna Loa is the largest volcano in the world. It is 2.6 miles above sea level. This enormous shield volcano covers half the island of Hawaii.

Cinder Cone Volcanoes

These volcanoes have steep slopes and wide craters at the top. They are formed by eruptions that shoot pieces of lava and ash into the air. These pieces of lava and ash are called cinders. The cinders pile up and form a cinder cone. These volcanoes can be formed by Strombolian eruptions.

Caldera Volcanoes

A large eruption can empty out the magma chamber under a volcano. When this happens, the part of the mountain above the chamber falls in. This creates a large crater called a caldera. Volcanoes with very large calderas are known as caldera volcanoes. Many calderas are formed by violent Plinian eruptions.

Cinder cones can be more than 800 feet high and 1,600 feet wide. They can occur in groups or near composite or shield volcanoes.

Crater Lake, in Oregon, lies in a caldera that is 6 miles wide. The caldera was formed when Mount Mazama erupted 7,000 years ago.

Types of Eruptions

Different volcanoes behave in different ways. The type of eruption affects the shape of the volcano. It also changes how the land and people around the volcano are affected.

Plinian Eruptions

Plinian eruptions are spectacular and dangerous. Gas-rich magma explodes. This sends gas, ash, and cinders into the sky. Plinian eruption plumes can be up to 28 miles high. Plinian eruptions can create pyroclastic flows that destroy everything in their path. Ash drifts for thousands of miles. The explosion can trigger landslides, mudslides, and floods.

Hawaiian Eruptions

Hawaiian eruptions are named after the Hawaiian Islands. Hawaiian eruptions are low-pressure events. The lava is less viscous. It flows slowly out of the volcano instead of exploding. Though slow, they are steady. Mount Kilauea has been erupting since 1983. It is one of the world's most active volcanoes.

Strombolian Eruptions

These eruptions are named after the island of Stromboli in the Mediterranean Sea. Many small bursts of thick lava, steam, and gas shoot into the air. They sometimes get as much as half a mile high. Stromboli itself erupts every 15–30 minutes. It sometimes throws blocks of lava into the air.

The 1991 Plinian eruption of Mount Pinatubo, in the Philippines, lasted nine hours.

Mount Kilauea has been erupting since 1983. This is its longest eruption in 500 years.

Stromboli has been erupting steadily for more than 2,000 years. Ancient Greek sailors used its glow to steer their ships.

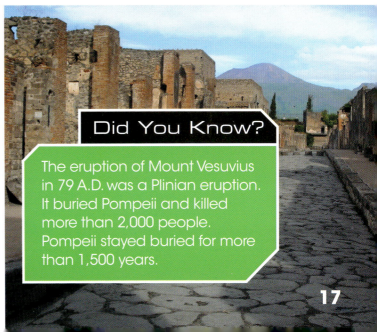

Did You Know?

The eruption of Mount Vesuvius in 79 A.D. was a Plinian eruption. It buried Pompeii and killed more than 2,000 people. Pompeii stayed buried for more than 1,500 years.

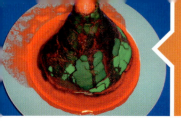

How to Make Your Own Volcano

You can make a volcano. Be careful! Erupting volcanoes are messy.

What You Need:
- an empty small plastic drink bottle
- modeling clay
- 1 cup white vinegar
- red food coloring and red glitter
- ½ cup water
- one heaping tablespoon baking soda

1 Pour vinegar into the bottle until it is one-third full. Add some red food coloring and glitter.

2 Wrap the bottle in clay to make it look like a real volcano. Put the bottle on a large plate or tray.

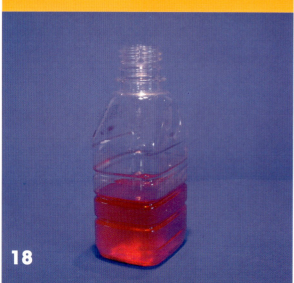

3 Mix the water and baking soda together in a separate container.

4 Pour this mixture into the bottle. Then watch your volcano erupt. What sort of volcanic eruption does it look like?

Making a Pyroclastic Flow

Pyroclastic flows are clouds of boiling hot gas and ash. They pour down the sides of a volcano at speeds of up to 100 miles an hour. They can reach temperatures of 1,300 degrees Fahrenheit.

Here's how to make a pyroclastic flow for your volcano. Repeat the steps, except this time add a few drops of dishwashing liquid to the vinegar in step 1. The frothy liquid that flows down the side of your volcano is similar to a pyroclastic flow.

Case Study— Mount St. Helens

On the morning of May 18, 1980, Mount St. Helens in Washington State erupted. The explosive eruption lasted for nine hours and killed 57 people. It devastated wildlife and the landscape.

The Mountain Stirs

Mount St. Helens had been quiet for over a century. In March 1980, small **tremors** and eruptions of gas and rock began. A bulge formed on its north side, which grew 450 feet high by mid-May. There were more tremors. Officials kept sightseers away.

The Mountain Explodes

On May 18, geologists were circling the **summit** in a small airplane. They saw the north face "ripple and churn" before it suddenly fell in. An enormous explosion followed. This blasted out millions of tons of rock and ash. An eruption plume rose 15 miles into the air.

The collapse triggered a landslide of 9 billion tons of rock and ice. The landslide reached speeds of 180 miles an hour.

The first blast traveled at least 300 miles an hour. The nine-hour eruption devastated 130,000 acres of land. It flattened everything for 7 miles to the north. Bolts of lightning flashed in the clouds of ash. Burning embers started over 300 forest fires.

In geological terms, the Mount St. Helens eruption was mild!

The Mount St. Helens blast was heard 200 miles away. The ash cloud spread across the United States in three days.

Did You Know?

The trees blown down by the eruption could have built 300,000 homes.

Before

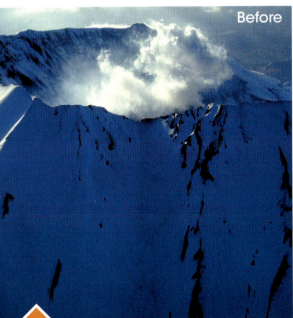

After

The explosive eruption blew away much of Mount St. Helens' summit. Its force was close to that of a 10-megaton hydrogen bomb. That's 500 times the power of the bomb dropped on Hiroshima at the end of World War II.

Volcanic Landscapes

*The areas around volcanoes are usually **geothermal** regions. The magma near Earth's surface heats the rocks around it. The rocks then heat the **groundwater** to high temperatures.*

Hot Springs

Hot springs are often found in geothermal regions. They form when heat from magma near the surface warms the rocks around it. The warm rocks then heat the groundwater. Water expands as it is heated. The expanding hot water forces its way to the surface. The water escapes as a hot spring.

Geysers

Geysers are hot springs that erupt from vents in the ground. They occur when groundwater becomes trapped in an underground chamber. Heat from nearby magma heats the trapped water. The water boils. It turns into steam. The steam builds up inside the chamber, which increases the pressure. Finally, the pressure becomes too great. It forces the water and steam up and out through a vent. They shoot high up into the air.

Mud Pots

Mud pots are created when hot steam and gases rise up through the Earth. They soften rock and mix with soil and ash. When surface water joins this mix, bubbling pools of hot mud form.

Did You Know?

The word *geyser* comes from the Icelandic language. It means "to gush, or rush forth."

Some geysers erupt very regularly. A geyser called "Old Faithful" in Yellowstone National Park erupts every hour or so.

The water in hot springs often contains minerals from the rocks it passed through. Some hot springs water is safe to drink.

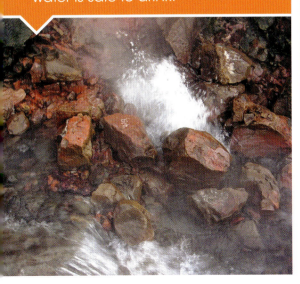

Some people believe that volcanic mud has healing powers.

Living with Volcanoes

People and volcanoes exist side by side all around the world. Volcanoes pose a threat. But living near volcanoes also has advantages.

Volcanic Soils

Volcanic soils are very **fertile**. This makes them good for growing crops. Indonesian farmers grow rice near active volcanoes. But their farms can be devastated by thick lava flows. It takes months for lava to cool and decades for soil to form.

Ancient Eruption, Modern Money Maker

Past eruptions provide daily benefits in Italy. The city Pompeii was buried when Mount Vesuvius erupted in 79 A.D. It now attracts thousands of visitors. These tourists bring in money that helps the local economy.

However, Mount Vesuvius is still active. Millions could be affected by a new eruption. Volcanic activity has brought benefits to southern Italy. But eruptions are always a threat.

Energy and Minerals

Groundwater heated by magma creates geothermal energy. Steam from hot groundwater can be used to make electrical power. Groundwater with a lower temperature can heat homes and supply bathing water. Geothermal energy is the second-largest source of electricity in Iceland.

Minerals are also useful **byproducts** of volcanic activity. Metals such as gold and copper are mined from the magma of extinct volcanoes after it has cooled and hardened.

Studies at Pompeii have taught us much about the lives of ancient Romans.

Geothermal energy around Svartsengi, Iceland, is used to produce electricity.

Mount Etna in Italy is Europe's highest active volcano.

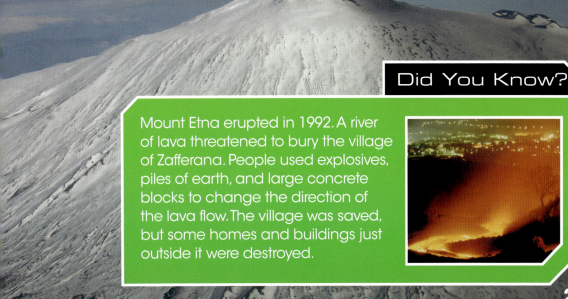

Did You Know?

Mount Etna erupted in 1992. A river of lava threatened to bury the village of Zafferana. People used explosives, piles of earth, and large concrete blocks to change the direction of the lava flow. The village was saved, but some homes and buildings just outside it were destroyed.

Working with Volcanoes

Volcanologists are scientists who study volcanoes. They try to find out how volcanoes form and predict when they might erupt.

Tuesday, 4:30 A.M.

Pasto, Colombia: I am up early. Low clouds will cover the summit of the Galeras volcano by mid morning. I'm taking two geology students with me today. I need to give them a health and safety talk once we're on the summit. Because of the students, I'll stick to the outer rim. We'll just take a few **core samples** and some readings with the seismograph.

9:00 A.M.

It's cold on the summit. It is strange how cool the air temperature is when the rocks I'm standing on are so hot. They would burn through the soles of a normal pair of boots. Mist and steam are swirling everywhere. The smell of sulfur is stronger than last week. We are all dressed in our protective gear now. It's time to get to work.

11:00 A.M.

We're back at the lower base camp. Today's readings were OK—three lava samples and some ground readings. The seismograph reported many small tremors. I've emailed the readings to the lab in Bogota. I will send the lava with the messenger tomorrow.

Even though the lava is hot, the air temperature is quite cool. I make sure to wear my heavy jacket.

Capturing the moment, I set up the camera to take a picture of the students.

Scientists cannot keep volcanoes from erupting. But they try to predict when an eruption will occur and how strong it will be. Their work helps to save lives.

Seismographs measure movements in the Earth. They help scientists predict when a volcano might erupt.

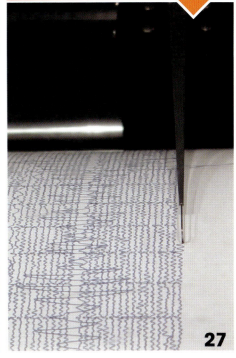

27

Time Line

Santorini, Greece
Huge eruption destroyed around 31 square miles of the island. Some believe this was the lost city of Atlantis.

Vesuvius, Italy
The ash from the eruption buried several Roman towns. They were not found for more than 1,500 years.

1620 B.C.　　　　　　　　　　　　　79 A.D.

Surtsey, Iceland
An underwater volcano created a new island. After ten days, it was 3,000 feet long and 1,100 feet wide. Three years after it stopped erupting, plants, insects, and birds were living on the island.

Paricutin, Mexico
A volcano sprung up in a cornfield overnight. It grew 550 feet in a week. After nine years of activity, it was 1,700 feet high.

1963　　　　　　　　　　　　　　1943

Heimaey, Iceland
One-third of the town was swallowed by a lava flow up to 20 feet deep. It added 1 square mile of land to the island.

Mount St. Helens, Washington
Explosion caused terrible damage to a beautiful mountain area of Washington State. It created 210 square miles of empty wasteland.

1973　　　　　　　　　　　　　　1980

Laki, Iceland
Lava covered 565 square miles of land. Its dust affected Europe, Africa, Asia, and North America, causing climate changes and famines. Largest lava flow in recorded history.

Tambora, Indonesia
Most powerful eruption in recorded history. Eighty times the power of Mount St. Helens. The following year in the Northern Hemisphere was called the "year without a summer."

1783   **1815**

Mount Pelee, Martinique, Caribbean
A huge pyroclastic flow claimed 30,000 lives. There were only two survivors.

Krakatoa, Indonesia
Much of the island collapsed into the sea. A resulting tsunami destroyed 165 villages. A later eruption created a new island.

1902   **1883**

Mount Ruiz, Colombia
Had not erupted for nearly 150 years. Mudslides buried four towns in the region. About 25,000 people were killed.

Pinatubo, Philippines
The largest eruption of the 20th century. The volcano had been dormant for more than 400 years. The eruption blocked out daylight in the area for days and blew off 500 feet of mountaintop.

1985   **1991**

Volcanoes and Eruptions

Type of Volcano	Type of Eruption	Volcanoes of the World
Composite	Plinian	Agua, Guatemala Hekla, Iceland Irazú Volcano, Costa Rica Klyuchevskaya, Russia Mount Cotopaxi, Ecuador Mount Fuji, Japan Mount Mayon, Luzon Mount Pinatubo, Philippines Mount Ruiz, Colombia Mount St. Helens, Washington
Cinder Cone	Strombolian	Amboy, California Cerro Negro, Nicaragua Heimaey, Iceland Paricutin, Mexico Red Cones, California Sunset Crater, Arizona Surtsey, Iceland
Shield	Hawaiian	Alcedo, Galapagos Islands Fernandina, Galapagos Islands Mauna Kea, Hawaii Mauna Loa, Hawaii Mount Kilauea, Hawaii
Caldera	Plinian	Krakatoa, Indonesia Santorini, Greece

Some volcanoes have more than one type of eruption.

Type of Volcano	Type of Eruption	Volcanoes of the World
Composite	Plinian/Strombolian Hawaiian/Plinian Hawaiian/Plinian/Strombolian Hawaiian/Plinian/Strombolian Hawaiian/Plinian/Strombolian	Mount Etna, Italy Mount Pelee, Caribbean Mount Vesuvius, Italy Stromboli, Italy Tambora, Indonesia

Glossary

byproducts (BY prod uhkts) things that are made in the process of doing something else

caldera (kal DEHR uh) a crater at the top of a volcano that is more than 1 kilometer (0.6 miles) across

cinder (SIHN duhr) a small piece of hot rock thrown into the air by a volcano

collide (kuh LYD) to crash together with a large amount of force

composite volcanoes (kuhm POZ iht vol KAY nohz) steep volcanoes formed by layers of lava and ash from explosive eruptions; also called stratovolcanoes

core samples (KOHR SAM puhls) samples taken from something, like a volcano or a tree, that show its layers in order to study it

crust (kruhst) the outer layer of Earth that is made up of solid rock

devastating (DEHV uh stay tihng) tending to cause complete destruction

erupts (ih RUHPTS) violently shoots something out

explosions (ehk SPLOH zhens) the actions of bursting with loud noises

fertile (FUR tuhl) able to grow many crops and other plants

geothermal (JEE uh THUR muhl) related to the heat inside the Earth

groundwater (GROWND WAWT uhr) water below the Earth's surface that feeds springs and wells

impact (IHM pakt) a forceful or dramatic effect

lahars (LAH hahrz) mudslides made up of water, ash, soil, and rock that are caused by volcanic eruptions

lava fountains (LAH vuh FOWN tuhns) jets of bright orange lava that shoot into the air like water from a fountain

magma (MAG muh) very hot melted rock that forms in the Earth's mantle

magma chamber (MAG muh CHAYM buhr) an underground space, usually under a volcano, where magma collects

mantle (MAN tuhl) the layer of partly melted rock below Earth's crust

molten (MOHL tuhn) melted

poisonous (POY zuh nihs) containing poison; very harmful to life and health

pressure (PREHS uhr) the continued action of a weight or force

pyroclastic flows (PY ruh KLAS tihk FLOHZ) clouds of boiling hot gas and ash that flow very quickly down the sides of volcanoes

subduction (suhb DUHK shuhn) the process of one tectonic plate colliding with and moving underneath another

summit (SUHM iht) the top or highest point on something, such as a mountain

tremors (TREHM uhrz) small vibrating movements of the earth

vents (vehntz) in a volcano, the openings in Earth's surface that lava or gases erupt through

viscosity (vihs KOS uh tee) the degree to which something is viscous, or very thick and sticky

Index

ash 5, 8–11, 14–16, 19–22, 28
caldera volcanoes 14–15, 30
cinder cone volcanoes 14–15, 30
composite volcanoes 14–15, 30
crater 9, 15, 30
Earth 4, 6, 10, 22, 27
Earth's crust 4, 6–7
eruption plume 10, 16, 20
eruptions 4, 8–10, 14–17, 19–21, 24, 27–30
gas 4, 8–10, 14, 16, 19–20, 22
geysers 22–23
Hawaii 7, 14, 30
Hawaiian eruptions 14, 16, 30
hot spots 6–7, 14
hot springs 22–23
lahars 10
land 4, 16, 20, 28–29
lava 4–5, 8–9, 14–16, 24–29
magma 4, 6–9, 14, 16, 22, 24
magma chamber 8–9, 15
mantle 6–7
molten 4, 6, 8
Mount St. Helens 9, 20–21, 28–30

mud pots 22
mudslides 4, 10, 16, 29
ocean 4, 6, 12–13
people 4, 10–11, 16–17, 20, 23–25, 29
Plinian eruptions 14–17, 30
pressure 6, 8–9, 14, 16, 22
pyroclastic flows 8, 16, 19, 29
Ring of Fire 13
scientists 26–27
seismograph 26–27
shield volcanoes 14–15, 30
spreading ridges 6–7, 14
Strombolian eruptions 15–16, 30
subduction 6–7
summit 20–21, 26
tectonic plates 6–7
tremors 20, 26
tsunamis 4, 29
vents 8–9, 22
Vesuvius 13, 17, 24, 28, 30
viscosity 8, 14, 16
volcanologist 26